MAURA VELLA

Manifesting Is Easy Peasy

Your Fun and Simple Guide to Achieving Anything You Want, Bit by Bit

First edition

This book was professionally typeset on Reedsy.
Find out more at reedsy.com

"Once you make a decision, the universe conspires to make it happen."

—Ralph Waldo Emerson

Contents

1

Introduction: What's the Buzz With Manifesting, Anyway?

Hey Friend! Welcome to *Manifesting Is Easy Peasy: Your Fun and Simple Guide to Achieving Anything You Want, Bit by Bit.* I know you might be thinking, "Manifesting? Isn't that just some kind of mysterious fluff for people with too much free time?" Well, think again. This book breaks down the art of manifesting into practical, bite-sized pieces that fit into even the busiest lifestyles. You found this book for a reason, which means you are exactly where you need to be, right here and right now. So keep reading and start your manifesting journey...

What is Manifesting?

Manifesting is like the magic key to life—it's the art of bringing your desires and dreams into reality by focusing your thoughts, feelings, and actions. It's not about waving a magic wand or just wishing on a star (though, let's be real, that would be cool as hell). Instead, it's about setting clear intentions and aligning yourself with what you want so the universe can give you a little nudge in the right direction. And guess what? It's not as complicated as it sounds.

Common Myths and Misconceptions

Let's clear the air on a few things. Manifesting isn't about sitting on your couch and hoping a million dollars will magically appear in your bank account. It's also not reserved for the super-spiritual or the ultra-zen. You don't need to meditate for hours or chant in a language you don't understand. This book will show you that anyone—yes, even you—can manifest, and it doesn't have to be weird or intimidating.

How To Use This Book

So, how do you navigate this magical journey? Easy Peasy. This book is your roadmap, filled with bite-sized chapters that break down manifesting into simple, actionable steps. No need to stress about "doing it right," just read along, and I'll guide you through the process. Think of it as an amusing experiment with your life as the lab. The best part? You don't have to wait long to see results—just a few minutes a day can make a huge difference.

A Bit of Psychology and Science

Throughout the book, I might toss in some psychology and science tidbits to show that this isn't just mystical mumbo jumbo. It's about how our brains work and how we can harness that power to create the life we want. We'll dip our toes into these principles just enough to keep things real without getting too deep into the academic side. Understanding a bit of the proven research on human behavior and the science behind manifesting can make the whole process feel a lot more grounded and practical.

Playful Approach with No Pressure

We're keeping things light and playful here. There's no pressure to be perfect or to manifest your dream life overnight. The goal is to have fun with it, experiment, and see what happens. Notice the small shifts, the little wins, and celebrate them. It's all about enjoying the journey, not just the destination.

Universal Concept

When I mention the universe, please don't get caught up on the term. You can refer to it in whatever way feels right to you—whether it's God, Source, Life Force, or something else entirely. The essence of what we're discussing is the recognition that there's a greater energy at work beyond our everyday lives. It's about connecting with that energy in a way that feels authentic and meaningful to you. The important thing is to embrace the idea that we're all part of something bigger, and that's the energy we're tapping into.

Practical Applications and Daily Practice

Each chapter will include easy, practical exercises that take no more than six minutes a day. That's right—just six minutes! Whether you're sipping your morning coffee or winding down at night, these practices are designed to fit seamlessly into your routine. Challenge yourself to try them out and watch how these small daily actions can lead to big changes.

By the end of this book, you'll have a solid understanding of what manifesting is and how to make it work for you. You'll also have a toolkit full of simple, effective techniques to help you start manifesting your desires. So, let's kick things off and dive into the next chapter, where I will lay down the rules of manifesting. Get ready to change your life, little by little.

2

Manifesting 101–The Ground Rules

Alright, fellow rule-bender, let's get real about the few essential guidelines you need to keep in mind for this manifesting journey. I know, rules are made to be broken sometimes, and I'm all for that. But here's the thing: a little structure helps, especially when you're just getting started. Think of these rules as the bumpers in a bowling alley. They're not there to box you in or ruin your excitement but to keep your ball rolling in the right direction. These guidelines are here to help you make the most out of manifesting, so don't throw them out the window entirely.

Don't Get Hooked on the Outcome

First things first: don't get too attached to the outcome. It may be easier said than done, but getting too fixated on how things *should* turn out leads to major dissatisfaction. It's like setting yourself up for disappointment if things don't go exactly as you pictured. When you're obsessed with the end result, you're basically telling the universe, "It's my way or the highway," which leaves little room for the unexpected magic that could happen.

It's like ordering at a restaurant. You have a general idea of what you want, but the details can surprise you. You might order a burger and get an unexpected but delightful side dish you hadn't imagined. If you're too focused on getting the exact meal you envisioned, you might miss out on enjoying the surprise. Focus on the feeling you want rather than the specific details. Instead of obsessing over that exact job title or dream house, tune into the emotions you want to experience—like feeling fulfilled, excited, or at peace. This way, you're open to a variety of ways those feelings can manifest, leaving space for even better outcomes than you imagined.

Let Go of the How

Once you've stopped obsessing over the endgame, it's easy to slip into the trap of obsessing over every single step to get there. This is a surefire way to stress yourself out and block all the cool, unexpected ways the universe can help you out.

Take the example of Wrigley's Chewing Gum. William Wrigley Jr. set out to build a successful business, but he had no clue that chewing gum would be his golden ticket. He started with soap and baking powder, throwing in a free pack of gum as a little bonus. But here's the twist—customers went nuts over the gum, way more than the main products.

Instead of sticking to his original plan, Wrigley listened to what the universe was telling him. He ditched the soap and baking powder and went all-in on gum. That pivot turned his small-time operation into a massive success. Wrigley's flexibility to adapt to what people actually wanted, rather than what he thought they should want, was the game-changer.

He didn't get stuck on how his business should look; he rolled with the unexpected demand for gum. This move didn't just meet his business goals—it blew them out of the water, showing that staying open to change can lead to way bigger wins than sticking to the original script.

Have you ever meticulously planned an event, only for everything to go completely off the rails? We've all been there— maybe it was a night out with friends or a big family gathering that didn't unfold as expected. But here's the thing: getting too caught up in every detail often blinds us to the unexpected magic that can happen when things don't go according to plan. When we avoid getting stuck in the "how" and stay open to the flow of the moment, we allow ourselves to experience joy and wonder in unexpected ways. Sometimes, the best experiences come from letting go of rigid expectations and embracing the surprises life throws our way. It's a reminder that magic often lies in the unplanned, in the moments we never saw coming, and that being flexible can lead to more fulfilling and memorable experiences.

Forget the Clock — Time's a Construct

Here's a mind-bender for you: in the world of manifesting, time is a bit of a cosmic joke. It's like the universe's way of saying, "Relax, I've got this." The whole concept of time as we know it—hours, days, deadlines—is something we humans cooked up to keep things organized here on Earth. The universe doesn't operate on our schedules, and that's perfectly fine.

In the manifesting universe, there's no rush, no ticking clock, and definitely no looming deadlines. The universe doesn't care about your calendar app or the reminders you set for yourself. It's on its own schedule, and sometimes that means things don't happen when you expect them to—or even when you want them to. But that's the beauty of it. Things unfold exactly when they're supposed to, in a way that serves your highest good. It might not be on your 9-to-5 schedule but trust that the universe knows best and is working things out behind the scenes.

Think of it like this: while we're down here stressing about minutes and hours, the universe is chilling in a timeless zone, arranging everything perfectly. So, if your big manifestation isn't showing up immediately, don't sweat it. The key is to stay patient, keep your vibe high, and trust that things are aligning in the best possible way. It's like waiting for a really good homemade pie—sometimes it takes a while, but when it's ready, it's absolutely worth it.

Spot the Small Wins and Boost Your Confidence

One of the coolest parts of manifesting is spotting those little signs and synchronicities that seem to pop up out of nowhere. It's like the universe giving you a sly wink. A wild concept that explains this is the Baader-Meinhof phenomenon, also known as the frequency illusion. It's that freaky thing where you learn about something new, and suddenly it feels like it's everywhere. It's not magic; it's your brain zeroing in on something it used to ignore.

Let's say you just found out about a funky breed of dog, like the Basenji. Before, you couldn't pick one out of a lineup, but now it feels like Basenjis are taking over the world. You see them at the park, in movies, even your friend's neighbor just got one. What the hell, right? This isn't just some cosmic joke—it's your brain tuning into what's been there all along. The universe is basically saying, "Hey, look! You're on the right track!"

You can mess around with this in your own life by picking something simple and random to notice—like red convertibles, pineapples, or the word "serendipity." Say you choose pineapples. Just think about noticing pineapples throughout your day. Don't get all worked up over it; just set the thought and carry on. You'll be amazed at how many times pineapples pop up—in the grocery store, on a shirt, or in a meme your friend sends you.

When you start seeing pineapples everywhere, don't just brush it off. Take it as a win. It's not really about the fruit; it's about proving to yourself that your focus can make stuff show up in your world. These little victories build your confidence in the whole manifesting deal. As you get better at spotting these signs, you'll feel more badass and ready to manifest bigger and cooler things. It's like working out a muscle—the more you flex it, the stronger it gets. These are the first steps in mastering your manifesting mojo!

Practical Application: Start Small and Keep It Light

Let's get you manifesting something simple to start with. Let's take a real-life example: I love playing this game with what I call my "princess parking spot." I've gotten so good at it that I almost always snag an awesome parking spot without even trying.

Here's how it works. Before I head out, I casually think about getting a spot close to the entrance of my destination, and nine times out of ten, there it is, waiting for me like a royal escort. It's not just luck; it's about setting the intention and letting the universe handle the rest. Try something like this out for yourself, whether it's your princess (or prince) parking spot or something else that's simple and fun. Maybe you want to get a free upgrade on your coffee order, hear your favorite song on the radio, or even get out of that one meeting that you aren't looking forward to, but you don't want to be the one who cancels it. Don't overthink it; just imagine it and then let it go. Whatever it is, keep it light and playful. When it happens, give yourself a little high-five and celebrate the win. This is just the beginning!

With these rules in mind, you're all set to dive deeper into the world of manifesting. Remember, it's all about keeping an open mind, trusting the process, and having fun along the way. Let's move on to the next chapter, where we'll talk about setting intentions and making the good stuff happen. Get ready!

3

Setting Intentions – Your Power Play

Setting intentions is like laying down the tracks for a train. You can't just throw a locomotive into the wild and hope it reaches its destination. You need a clear path and a sense of direction. In this chapter, we're diving into the nitty-gritty of how to get crystal clear on what you actually want. Vague desires lead to vague results, so let's get specific and set the foundation for your manifesting journey.

Get Clear on What You Want

First things first, you've got to define what you want—and I mean really define it. No half-assed, surface-level wishes here. We're talking about digging deep and getting to the core of your desires. Keep in mind that oftentimes what we think we want isn't really the end goal, but a means to something more meaningful. For example, you might say you want a new job, but what you're really seeking is more freedom and less stress. Or maybe you're dreaming of a bigger house, but it's actually the desire for a comfortable and safe space that's driving you. By getting specific about what you truly want, you can focus your energy more effectively.

Also, don't hesitate to admit what you truly want, even if it seems far-fetched or unconventional. Maybe you've always envisioned yourself owning a private island, despite having a modest income and no experience in real estate. We often shy away from our biggest dreams, fearing they're too wild or because we feel undeserving. But here's the truth: you deserve whatever you can dream of. This clarity in setting your intentions is key to manifesting. And don't worry—we're going to give you the tools to peel back those layers and uncover what really lies beneath your desires.

Dig Into Your Why

It's time to play psychologist for a minute and figure out why the hell you want it. Don't worry, this isn't a deep therapy session— just a quick self-assessment. Something to note: the "why" behind what you want isn't about ticking off boxes to impress others or adhering to what society thinks you should do. Nope, that's their business. This, on the other hand, is all about you. So, ask yourself: Why do you care about this goal or dream? What's the real deal behind it?

Understanding your motivations is like adding rocket fuel to your manifesting fire. It taps into those basic human needs that we all have, whether we like to admit it or not. For instance, many of us crave a sense of security and safety. Maybe your goal of buying a private island isn't just about owning a secluded paradise; perhaps it's about the ultimate freedom and escape from the hustle and bustle of everyday life. It's not just about having a luxury retreat; it might be the dream of creating a personal sanctuary where you can truly be yourself, far away from the demands and judgments of society. Or maybe the island represents the freedom to live life on your terms, creating a unique space to share with loved ones and connecting on a deeper level away from the distractions of modern life.

Whatever your reasons are, own them. The more you understand your true motivations, the more fire you'll have to chase after your dreams. And remember, your "why" isn't just a guide; it's your personal cheerleader, keeping you pumped up and on track, no matter what life throws your way.

Feel It to Believe It

Feelings are the engine of manifesting. They drive your actions and focus, guiding your manifestations. When you connect with the emotions of achieving your goals, you set the direction for the universe to bring those experiences into your life. Let's zero in on that dream of owning a private island. Picture stepping off the boat, feeling the warm sand under your feet, and the sea breeze brushing your face. It all feels so good and relaxing. This is a place where you can relax and truly be yourself, far away from the noise and expectations of everyday life.

As you envision this island, think about the emotions it stirs. Is it the exhilarating sense of freedom, knowing you can escape to your sanctuary whenever you want, free to choose? Or perhaps it's the profound peace and relaxation of having a space that's entirely your own, where every palm tree and wave crashing on the shore is a reminder of the life you've built. Maybe it's the pride and accomplishment of creating a unique space that reflects your vision and desires.

Let all of these feelings wash over you as if you're already living that island life. Feel the joy of waking up to the sound of the waves, the thrill of exploring your domain, and the contentment of knowing you've created a life of your own making. These emotions are your compass, pointing you toward your manifestations. The more vividly you can imagine and feel these emotions, the stronger your signal to the universe. So dive deep into those feelings of freedom, autonomy, and joy, and let them be the force that guides your manifesting journey.

What Will You Get Out of This?

Now, let's switch gears from the feel-good vibes to the real-world perks of achieving your goals. While the last section was all about tapping into the emotions, this one focuses on the concrete, practical outcomes.

Let's go back to our private island example. Beyond the joy and excitement of owning a slice of paradise, there are several tangible benefits. First up is the undeniable sense of accomplishment. It's not just about saying, "I did it"—it's about seeing the results of your efforts in a real, physical form. It's like a badge of honor that boosts your confidence and shows you can turn dreams into reality.

Then there's the financial upside. Owning an island isn't just a whimsical escape; it's a valuable asset that could increase in value over time. This kind of investment offers a layer of financial security, whether you plan to develop it, rent it out, or sell it later. It's like having a big, beautiful safety net that can support other dreams and ventures.

And let's not forget the practical freedom that comes with such an achievement. This isn't just about feeling free; it's about having actual, tangible choices. Whether you want to throw epic beach parties, create a secluded retreat, or just have a place to chill out and escape whenever life gets too hectic, the island gives you the literal space to do it. It's the embodiment of living life on your terms.

Understanding these real-world benefits helps keep your eye on the prize. So as you set your intentions and start manifesting, remember both the emotional and practical gains. This balanced perspective will keep you motivated and grounded, helping you navigate any bumps along the way.

The Magic of Writing It Down

Writing down your intentions isn't just a simple act; it's a powerful tool that can help turn your dreams into reality. It's like making a pact with the universe, saying, "This is what I want, and I'm ready for it." By being specific and clear, you're not just throwing wishes into the air; you're setting a focused, intentional path for what you want to manifest.

One of my favorite and simplest examples of the power of writing down specific intentions is Jim Carrey's story. Before he became a household name, Jim Carrey was a struggling actor trying to make it in Hollywood. In 1990, while he was struggling as a starving artist, he decided to make his intentions tangible. He wrote himself a check for $10 million for "acting services rendered" and dated it for Thanksgiving 1995. He kept this check in his wallet as a constant reminder of his goal.

At that time, writing a check for $10 million might have seemed like a far-fetched dream for Carrey, who was facing rejection and financial challenges. Yet, this simple act of writing down a clear and specific intention served as a powerful motivator and focus point. It wasn't just a wish; it was a tangible, visual representation of his aspiration.

Fast forward to 1994, just before Thanksgiving, and Jim Carrey learned that he would be paid $10 million for his role in Dumb and Dumber. This wasn't a random stroke of luck; it was the culmination of years of hard work, belief in himself, and a clear vision of what he wanted to achieve. Carrey's story is a compelling example of how writing down specific goals can help focus your energy and actions, ultimately leading to their realization.

By simply writing down his intention, Jim Carrey was able to keep his goal at the forefront of his mind, pushing him to take the necessary steps to achieve it. This story illustrates how a simple action like jotting down a goal can set the stage for incredible outcomes. If you haven't tried it yet, start with something small and see how it unfolds. It's about setting a clear intention and watching the universe respond.

The Trick Is to Be Open

When setting intentions, it's crucial to understand that the goal isn't to lock yourself into one specific outcome. The trick is not to expect that private island exactly as you envisioned it but rather to stay open to the essence of what that island represents.

Maybe the island isn't a literal one but a beautiful beach house where you can retreat and find peace, or a serene lakeside cabin offering the same escape from daily stress, or even a tranquil home office setup that provides a space to disconnect and relax. Perhaps it's the financial freedom to take regular vacations to various islands, experiencing the thrill of new places on the water while enjoying the calm and beauty of nature. Each scenario offers feelings of freedom, sanctuary, and connection, just in a different form. By staying open, you allow the universe to deliver what you truly need, often in ways even better than you imagined.

Practical Application: Pen It Down

Grab a journal, a sticky note, your phone, or even scribble it on a napkin—the important thing is to get your thoughts out of your head and onto something tangible. Follow these three easy steps:

Write down what you want: Be specific about your goal or desire. It can be as big or as small as you like. List out three aspects below your intention:

- Why: Identify why you want this. What's the underlying

reason or motivation?
- Feel: How will achieving this goal make you feel? What emotions will it bring?
- Provides: What will achieving this goal provide for you? What are the tangible or intangible benefits?

Next, fill in no more than 10 words for each aspect. Keep it concise and to the point.

Example:

Let's say you're dreaming of buying that private island. Here's how you'll write it all down.

- *What I want: To buy a private island*
- *Why: To reduce the busyness from daily life and find peace*
- *Feel: Freedom and relaxation*
- *Provides: A personal retreat, investment, and creative space*

This exercise helps you gain clarity and focus, making it easier to bring your manifestation magic to life. Keep this memo visible to stay aligned with your intentions. Writing down your goals isn't just a ritual; it's a powerful way to set the wheels in motion and get you in sync with your desires. So, jot it down, get specific, and believe that you will receive the gifts from the universe.

4

Visualize Your Dream Life

Visualization is like daydreaming with a purpose. Many of us spend a significant amount of time mentally replaying past mistakes or worrying about potential negative outcomes. This kind of mental rehearsal of negative events can sap our energy and keep us stuck in a cycle of regret and anxiety.

But what if we flip that script? Instead of using our mental energy to relive the past or dread the future, we can redirect it toward creating a vision of the amazing possibilities ahead. This chapter invites you to harness the power of visualization, not to rehash what's gone wrong, but to imagine what's possible and exciting in your future. By consciously choosing to focus on positive outcomes and dreams, we can transform the way we think and feel, opening up new paths and opportunities. It's all about using the same energy we often waste on worry and regret to paint a picture of our ideal future and make it a reality.

The Brain Science Behind It

Before we dive into the how-to, let's talk science. And yes, I know I've been all about the good vibes and energy flow, but bear with me—this is cool stuff. Neuroscience (i.e. science of our brain) shows that when we visualize an activity, we activate the same brain regions as when we physically perform that activity. It's like giving your brain a mental dress rehearsal, prepping it for the real thing.

Here's the scoop: your brain can't quite tell the difference between a real experience and a vividly imagined one. When you visualize, you're essentially tricking your brain into thinking you're actually doing the thing you're imagining. This activates neural pathways and can improve skills, increase motivation, and boost confidence. It's a technique used by elite athletes, like when a basketball player visualizes sinking a free throw or a skier imagines a perfect run. They use this mental practice to enhance their actual performance, and it works. Studies have shown that athletes who visualize their performance often perform better than those who don't. It's all about creating a mental blueprint that primes your body and mind for success.

So, even though I might seem like I'm getting all sciency on you, it's because there's practicality to this whole visualization thing. It's not just about dreaming—it's about setting your brain up for real-world success. And hey, if it's good enough for Olympic champions, it's good enough for us mere mortals aiming to nail a presentation or land that promotion.

The Do's and Don'ts

Let's dive into the essentials of making your visualization practice truly powerful. When it comes to visualization, there are a few key rules to keep in mind to make your mental imagery as effective as possible. Think of these tips as your roadmap to manifesting your desires with clarity and precision. The more vividly and accurately you visualize, the more potent your visualization practice will be. These are the foundational principles that will take your daydreams from "nice thought" to "holy crap, it's happening!" So, grab your imagination and let's establish these core guidelines.

No How, Just What:
Here's the deal: when visualizing, focus on what you want, not how you're going to get it. The "how" is the universe's job— let it do its thing. Your job is to zero in on the end result. For instance, if you're dreaming about that perfect beach house, don't sweat the details of the mortgage or the real estate market. Instead, see yourself lounging on the deck, soaking up the sun, and listening to the waves. The universe will figure out the rest, so stop stressing and just visualize the dream.

Listen, I know that it's super easy to get stuck on the "how." We're naturally inclined to want to control every step, but doing so can limit the infinite possibilities available. This rule can be a tricky one to follow, but it's crucial. Trust that the universe has a better plan than you could imagine and resist the urge to micromanage the process. (Hmmm... do you micromanage any other parts of your life too?) Focus solely on the end result, and let the universe handle the logistics. So, let go, and let the universe surprise you with the how.

Pretend It's Already Happened:
Act as if you've already achieved your goal. This isn't about faking it until you make it; it's about immersing yourself in the experience. Picture every detail. What do you see? Who's there celebrating with you? How does your body feel—are you relaxed, energized, over the moon? For example, if you're visualizing acing a job interview, see yourself walking out of the building with a confident smile, shaking hands with your new boss, and feeling that triumphant rush of nailing it.

Engage All Your Senses:
Make your visualizations as multi-sensory as possible. Don't just see it—hear it, smell it, taste it, feel it. If you're dreaming of a killer meal at a fancy restaurant, don't just see the plate. Hear the clinking of silverware, smell the delicious aroma, feel the texture of the food in your mouth, and taste the exquisite flavors. This full-sensory approach makes the experience more vivid and convincing to your brain.

Feel the Emotions:
As we discussed earlier, emotions bring the juice. When imagining your desired outcome, don't just picture it—feel it. Whether it's joy, relief, pride, or excitement, dive into those emotions. If you're visualizing winning an award, feel the pride swelling, the thrill in your veins, and the warmth of the spotlight. These emotions make your visualization vivid and align your actions with your goals.

Keep It Positive

Stay on the sunny side. Visualize positive outcomes only. This isn't about ignoring potential challenges; it's about setting a positive tone for your mental rehearsal. If you're anxious about an upcoming presentation, don't visualize tripping over your words. Instead, see yourself delivering your points smoothly, with the audience nodding along and clapping at the end. Your brain doesn't know the difference between a real and imagined experience, so feed it the good stuff.

By following these rules, you're not just daydreaming—you're creating a mental blueprint that your brain and the universe can work with. The more vividly and positively you visualize, the more you're setting yourself up for success. So, get detailed, get emotional, and most importantly, have fun with it. The future you're dreaming of is just a few mental pictures away.

Practical Application: Daily Visualization Exercise

Now that you understand the power of visualization, let's put it into practice with a simple daily exercise. This exercise is quick, easy, and designed to set a positive tone for your day. Here's what you need to do:

- Start Your Day with a 2 Minute Visualization: Before getting out of bed, spend two minutes visualizing your day. (And hey, if you don't get a chance to do it when you wake up because you're tending to a sick dog, do it when you can get just 2 minutes to yourself.) Picture yourself with everyday events going smoothly, like having a pleasant conversation, having a great workout, or enjoying a quiet moment with a cup of tea. The key is to focus on positive outcomes and feel the emotions that come with these experiences.

- Next Level Trick To Mix It Up: While you're at it, mix in some bigger life desires. Imagine something grand like going on your dream vacation, landing your ideal job, or meeting the love of your life. Picture every detail and get into your senses and emotions. Immerse yourself in the joy of that achievement.

Remember, the goal is to make this a regular practice, not a chore. Whether you visualize small wins or big dreams, the important part is consistency. Even if some days you feel as if you only have a brief moment instead of the full 2 minutes to imagine—just do it. That's still mindfulness and you're doing great!

Pro Tip: Set a timer for two minutes to keep yourself on track

* * *

"The best way to find yourself is to lose yourself in the service of others."— Mahatma Gandhi

Spread the Magic of Manifesting

Hey, fellow Manifestor! You already know that good vibes and generosity create more of the same. So, let's put that into action—together!

Would you help someone just like you—curious about manifesting but unsure where to start? My mission is to make manifesting easy, fun, and ridiculously doable for everyone (yes, even the skeptics).

But here's the thing—most people choose books based on reviews. So, I need your help. Your review isn't just about this book—it's about paying it forward. It takes less than a minute, costs nothing, but could completely change someone's journey. Your review might be the reason...

✧ One more person finally *gets* manifesting.

✧ One more skeptic gives it a shot—and is blown away.

✧ One more dream actually comes true.

✧ One more person learns simple, actionable steps to create the life of their dreams.

It's super easy: Just scan the QR code below or go to this link to leave your review: https://www.amazon.com/review/create-review/?asin=B0DC8KPF23

If putting more positivity into the world feels right to you, then you're already a rockstar in my book. Thank you so much!

-Maura Vella

5

Get Your Mindset Right

The Law of Attraction has become quite the buzz phrase lately, and for good reason. It's the idea that like attracts like— essentially, the energy you put out into the universe is what you attract back to you. Think of it as the universe's way of saying, "You get what you give." And while this sounds fine and dandy, we should clear up some misconceptions right off the bat. The Law of Attraction isn't about effortlessly getting everything you desire without lifting a finger. We're not talking about magical thinking here. The Law of Attraction is about aligning your thoughts, feelings, and actions with your goals, creating a conducive environment for them to materialize.

At its core, the Law of Attraction suggests that your thoughts and emotions have a specific energy or vibration. When you're thinking positively and feeling good, you're like a magnet attracting positive experiences and opportunities. Just like a magnet aligns with metal objects, your "good vibes only" signal draws in all the good stuff you desire. Conversely, if you're stuck in a negative mindset, it's like flipping the polarity of the magnet—you start attracting more negative experiences, pulling in all the things you'd rather avoid. Your mindset essentially sets the polarity of your magnetic field, determining whether you attract positive or negative experiences based on the energy you're putting out.

Here's where more psychology hacks can come into play, particularly with the concept of confirmation bias. This nifty little mental trick means our brains are wired to notice and remember things that confirm what we already believe. If you believe that "Good things always happen to me," your brain will highlight every positive event, from finding a perfect parking spot to receiving unexpected compliments. Your brain becomes your personal cheerleader, reinforcing your positive beliefs and keeping that magnetic field buzzing with good energy. Conversely, if you're convinced that "Nothing ever goes right for me," you'll only notice the setbacks and ignore the positives, which makes you feel like you're perpetually under a dark cloud. This selective focus on the negatives just strengthens the negative magnet, attracting even more of what you don't want. So as you can see, it's important to know how your thoughts and beliefs shape your reality.

While the Law of Attraction might have a mystical vibe, there's a practical aspect grounded in how our brains work. It's about mindfulness and conscious intention. Focusing on positive outcomes and maintaining a positive mindset helps bring those outcomes into reality, actively setting your mental magnet to attract them. Whether you lean towards a spiritual or logical explanation, the key takeaway is the same: your mindset matters. Be intentional with your thoughts, keep your energy positive, and align your actions with the good things you want to attract. As you do this, you'll notice how the universe responds, delivering opportunities and experiences that resonate with your positive energy. Keep those positive vibes strong and let the Law of Attraction work its magic in bringing your aspirations to life.

Think Big — Abundance vs. Scarcity

Let's dive into the concept of Abundance vs. Scarcity with a bit of science flair. Have you ever heard that the universe is constantly expanding? It's not just a metaphor; it's a scientific fact. Since the Big Bang, the universe has been creating more space, more possibilities, and more of everything. This concept of constant expansion perfectly illustrates abundance—always growing, always making room for new opportunities, resources, and experiences.

Now, imagine if the universe operated with a scarcity mindset and thought, "There's only so much space, and we better not expand too much." It sounds absurd, right? Yet, a scarcity mindset works similarly. It's the belief that resources are limited and that someone else's gain is your loss. This mindset breeds competition, anxiety, and jealousy, causing people to hoard what they have and be reluctant to share, fearing there won't be enough. It's like trying to live in a shrinking universe, constantly feeling the walls close in.

The universe doesn't limit itself, and neither should we. Having an abundance mindset means believing there's enough for everyone—whether it's money, love, success, or opportunities. It's about seeing the world as full of endless possibilities, where good things are always available and more is always on the way. I know that's a big concept to wrap your head around, but let it sink in. Because it's the truth.

To embrace an abundance mindset, recognize that life is expansive and full of limitless opportunities. Just as the universe continually expands, life offers new chances and resources. Shifting your focus from scarcity to abundance opens you up to infinite possibilities. This doesn't mean ignoring challenges or limits; it's about understanding that these limits can expand and that there's always room for more good in your life. Believing in the constant growth of possibilities is key to thriving, not just surviving, in an ever-expanding universe of opportunities.

The Gratitude Game

We can't talk about abundance without mentioning its cousin, gratitude. It's easy to overlook, but gratitude is like the ultimate life hack. Not only does it make you feel good, but it also shifts your focus from what's lacking to what's abundant in your life. When you focus on what you're thankful for, you're essentially telling the universe, "Hey, I'm loving this! More of this, please!" It's like tuning your radio to a frequency of positivity, and suddenly, all the good stuff starts flowing your way.

Here's the thing: gratitude isn't just a feel-good practice; it's a lens through which we view the world, allowing us to see and appreciate the good in every situation, even when things aren't perfect. Did you get stuck in traffic but ended up listening to your favorite podcast? That's something to be grateful for. Found a dollar in your pocket? Celebrate that small win! These little moments of appreciation create a ripple effect, attracting even more reasons to be thankful.

Now, before you roll your eyes and think, "Yeah, yeah, another gratitude spiel," let's get real. Practicing gratitude doesn't mean ignoring the bad stuff or pretending everything's perfect. It's about acknowledging the good amidst the chaos. It's about finding that silver lining, no matter how thin it may be. And the best part? It's scientifically proven to boost your mood and overall well-being. So, not only are you manifesting more good things, but you're also getting a natural happiness boost—talk about a win-win!

Here's how it works: when you express gratitude, you're essentially sending out positive energy. Remember that whole "like attracts like" thing? Well, gratitude is a powerful magnet. The more you appreciate what's already in your life, the more you'll attract things to be grateful for. It's like a cosmic game of "thank you" tag—once you start, the universe can't help but keep it going.

Gratitude is like a magic wand that helps you find a little glimmer in any situation. It's not just about saying "thank you" for the big wins but also for those little things that make life sweeter, like a perfect cup of coffee or a gorgeous sunny day. It's about keeping your eyes peeled for the often-overlooked moments that make you smile. The more you embrace gratitude, the more it becomes second nature, and trust me, your life will start to glow a little brighter with every "thank you" you send out into the world.

Busting Limiting Beliefs and Fears

So, you've got your abundance mindset tuned in, and you're ready to attract all the good stuff. But then, like an uninvited guest, those sneaky limiting beliefs and fears show up, crashing your manifesting party. It's time to show them the door because overcoming these mental blocks is crucial to unlocking your full potential and truly embracing an abundant life.

Limiting beliefs are those pesky, negative thoughts that whisper, "You can't do that," or "You're not good enough." They often stem from past experiences, societal conditioning, or even well-meaning but misguided advice from others. These beliefs can be deeply ingrained, lurking in the back of your mind, sabotaging your efforts to move forward. For example, maybe you've always believed that "money is the root of all evil," or "success is only for the lucky." These thoughts aren't just annoying; they're downright destructive, holding you back from reaching your full potential.

Fear often partners with these limiting beliefs to keep you stuck. Fear of failure, fear of success, fear of the unknown—these fears can paralyze you, stopping you from taking the necessary steps toward your goals. It's like standing at the edge of a diving board, knowing the water's fine but being too scared to jump. Fear can be a powerful emotion, but it doesn't have to control you. The trick is to acknowledge it, understand it, and then move past it.

To overcome these limiting beliefs and fears, the first step is to identify them. Call them out and expose them for what they are—unfounded assumptions, not facts. Once you've identified them, challenge them. Fact check. Ask yourself, "Is this belief really true?" "Where did it come from?" Next, it's time to find some evidence that contradicts this belief. This takes a little practice, but give it a try. For instance, if you believe "I'm not good enough," find instances in your life where you've succeeded, excelled, or received praise. These counter-examples are proof that your limiting beliefs are not the whole truth.

Now, replace these limiting beliefs with empowering ones. Turn "I can't" into "I can," and "I'm not good enough" into "I am more than enough." It might feel a bit cheesy at first, but you can rewire your brain over time by simply replacing the limiting thoughts with possibilities. (More on this in the next section.)

By identifying, challenging, and replacing your limiting beliefs and facing your fears head-on, you'll start dismantling the barriers that hold you back. This isn't about ignoring reality or pretending challenges don't exist; it's about choosing to see possibilities and taking action toward them. Remember, your mind is like a garden—weed out the limiting beliefs and fears, and make room for positive thoughts and actions to flourish. The more you practice, the more natural it becomes, and before you know it, you'll be living in a world of your own limitless potential.

Boost Yourself with Positive Affirmations

As you work on overcoming limiting beliefs and fears, it's essential to fill that mental space with empowering and positive thoughts. Enter affirmations, your new best friends in building a more positive mindset. I know, repeating positive statements to yourself might feel a bit awkward or even silly at first. You might think, "Is this really doing anything?" But trust me, it's working. It's all about reprogramming your subconscious mind to support you rather than sabotage you. It's like giving your brain a pep talk, reminding it of what's possible and what you're capable of.

Affirmations are like mental reset buttons. They help you shift from a mindset of doubt and limitation to one of confidence and possibility. By consistently repeating these positive, specific statements, you're essentially re-training your brain to focus on what you want to achieve, rather than what you're afraid of. It's not just about spouting off wishful thinking; it's about creating a new internal dialogue that aligns with your goals and aspirations.

Let's revisit the example from the limiting beliefs section, where you might have thought, "I'm not good enough." This belief can be a major roadblock, keeping you from pursuing opportunities or taking risks because deep down, you don't feel deserving. But here's where affirmations come into play. Instead of letting that negative belief run the show, you can actively replace it with an empowering one. Turn "I'm not good enough" into "I am more than enough." This may be hard, but I really want you to take a second to feel the truth of those words. You are beginning to rewire your brain by replacing the limiting thoughts with possibilities. And over time, as you consistently replace the negative with the positive, you'll find that your confidence grows, and your actions start to reflect this new belief.

Think of it like reprogramming a computer. Your mind has been running on outdated software (those limiting beliefs), and affirmations are like installing a new, upgraded operating system. This new system helps you process information differently, react to challenges more constructively, and see opportunities where you might have previously seen obstacles.

And yes, we're getting a bit psychological here! This technique is actually rooted in cognitive-behavioral therapy (CBT), which is all about identifying and challenging negative thought patterns and replacing them with positive ones. So, not only are you diving into some powerful self-help, but you're also dabbling in a little DIY psychology. You're basically your own therapist now—you're welcome!

Practical Application: Develop a Positive Mindset

Let's keep this quick and easy, because who has time for complicated morning routines? Here's your simple, no-fuss guide to starting your day on a high note:

- Morning High-Five: First things first, give yourself a high-five in the mirror. Yep, just do it. It's silly, it's fun, and it's a great way to kick off your day with some positive energy. (Thanks to Mel Robbins and her High5Habit for this daily

feel-good hack!)
- Write Down Three Affirmations: Grab a sticky note, journal, or your phone—whatever's handy. Write down any three affirmations that resonate with you. They can be the same each day, or you can mix them up. The trick is to keep them short, sweet, and to the point. Here are a few guidelines:

1. Present Tense: Use phrases like "I am confident" instead of "I will be confident."
2. Positive Language: Focus on the positive. Say, "I am calm and relaxed," not "I am not stressed."
3. Be specific and Believable. Rather than "I am successful," try "I am thriving in my career and loving it."

- End-of-Day Glance: Before you hit the sack, take a quick look at your affirmations. Reflect on how these positive statements influenced your day. Did they help you feel more confident? More at ease? This quick check-in helps reinforce the positive mindset you're building.

This daily affirmation routine is like your morning coffee—best served daily for maximum effect. But let's get one thing straight: this isn't about being perfect. We're not aiming for some unrealistic, 100% flawless record of doing it every single day. Life happens. Sometimes you miss a day, and that's okay. The goal here is consistency, not perfection. So, show up for yourself as often as you can, and watch how these small daily actions start to shift your mindset and bring more positivity into your life.

6

Move Your Butt: Inspired Action

I hate to sound like a broken record, but I'm going to say it again: manifesting isn't just about sitting around and waiting for things to fall into your lap. Yes, I know, we've covered this, but it's worth repeating because it's so crucial. Effort is an integral part of the manifesting equation, and no, effort doesn't mean hard work or hours of toil. It's about making consistent, intentional moves towards your goals. Think of it as flexing a new muscle; at first, it might feel awkward, but with practice, it becomes second nature. But you've got to start somewhere and just do the thing. And as we've already discussed, sometimes these actions are as quick and simple as a 2 second hack.

The Action Factor — Make It Happen

The Law of Action is a crucial element in the art of manifesting your desires, and yes, it's another universal law in this cosmic playbook. While the Law of Attraction deals with the vibes you send out and what you draw into your life through thoughts and feelings, the Law of Action is about the moves you make to turn those vibes into reality. It's like having a dance partner; you might set the rhythm with your intentions and visualizations, but the universe can't lead the dance if you don't take the steps.

Think of it this way: dreaming about becoming a painter is great, but until you actually pick up a brush and start painting, you're just daydreaming. The Law of Action is your signal to get off your butt and start moving towards your goals. It's not about wearing yourself out with endless tasks; it's about taking intentional and inspired steps that align with what you want. Whether it's enrolling in an art class, buying a set of paints, or dedicating time to practice, these actions are what bring your dreams into the tangible world.

Every little action you take builds momentum, much like a dance where each step naturally leads to the next. It's as if the routine was masterfully choreographed, yet it unfolds spontaneously, with each movement flowing effortlessly into the next. This dance comes together in a way that feels both intentional and organic, creating a harmonious blend of movements that appear seamless but are powerfully impactful. Similarly, when you take small, consistent actions, they interconnect and build upon each other, making your dreams not only possible but increasingly tangible. It's like watching your life transform into a beautifully unfolding dance, perfectly aligned with your desires.

To put it simply: manifesting is like a dance between you and the universe. You set the intention and rhythm, and the universe follows your lead, bringing opportunities and outcomes into your life. Your actions make this dance come alive. The Law of Action is about making those initial moves and staying in sync, even when progress feels slow. Every step you take brings you closer to your dreams, and the universe loves a partner who's willing to dance. So, take the lead and let the Law of Action turn your intentions into reality.

Spot and Seize Opportunities

OK! You've set your intentions and are taking inspired actions. Now, it's time to sharpen your radar for opportunities because the universe loves to throw them your way when you least expect them. Recognizing and acting on these opportunities is like playing a game of cosmic hide-and-seek—except the universe is your partner, leaving little clues everywhere.

Picture this: you're on a treasure hunt. Your map is your intentions, and your tools are the actions you're taking. The real treasure, though, is in spotting those shiny opportunities that pop up along the way. They might come disguised as a random chat with someone in line at Target, a job opening you stumble upon online, or a sudden idea that hits you out of nowhere. The trick is to stay open and alert, ready to pounce on these chances when they appear.

But here's the kicker—acting on these opportunities often means stepping out of your comfort zone. It's that mix of intuition and guts that pushes you to say yes, even when the path ahead isn't crystal clear, because not every opportunity will come with a flashing neon sign. In fact, sometimes they might look like roadblocks or detours. Maybe you didn't get that promotion you were gunning for. Sure, it stings, but what if that setback is actually a nudge towards a more fulfilling career path you hadn't considered? The universe has a funny way of rerouting us to where we're supposed to be, often through unexpected twists and turns.

The key here is flexibility. If you're too fixated on one particular outcome, you might miss out on other awesome possibilities. Keep an open mind, and be willing to pivot when the universe sends you in a new direction. It's about rolling with the punches and seeing the big picture.

In a nutshell, recognizing and acting on opportunities is all about staying tuned in and ready to move. It's about jumping on those chances, even when they come wrapped in strange packaging or require a leap of faith. Remember, each opportunity is like a stepping stone, guiding you closer to your dreams. So, stay sharp, stay flexible, and be ready to grab the universe's offerings with both hands.

Mastering Patience and Persistence

Balancing patience and persistence in manifesting is like tending a garden. Persistence is all about planting the seeds, watering them regularly, and making sure they get enough sunlight. It's the consistent effort you put in, nurturing your dreams day by day. Patience, on the other hand, is knowing that you can't rush nature. You can't force the flowers to bloom before they're ready; they will blossom in their own time. You have to trust that, beneath the soil, things are happening even if you can't see them yet. So, while you're diligently watering and weeding, you're also waiting and trusting that your garden will eventually flourish.

Remember when we talked about the concept of time earlier? How it's more of a human construct, and the universe operates on its own timeline? Well, this is where that concept really comes into play. Persistence means sticking with your actions, even when things seem slow. It's like being a gardener: you plant the seeds (your intentions and actions), water them (keep up with your efforts), and then you wait. You don't sit there staring at the dirt, stressing about when the sprout will appear. You trust that something is happening beneath the surface.

Patience, on the other hand, is about not freaking out when things don't happen immediately. It's about understanding that sometimes the universe needs a little time to align everything perfectly for you. Just because you can't see progress doesn't mean it isn't happening. Maybe the job offer you want is still being drafted, or the perfect partner is finishing up their last bad date before finding you. Patience is about trusting that the universe has your back and that things are unfolding in the perfect time.

Now, here's where it gets tricky. If you're constantly checking your watch, metaphorically speaking, and stressing over why things aren't happening yet, you're putting a chokehold on your manifestations. It's like trying to force a cake to bake faster by cranking up the heat—you'll just end up burning it. Instead, focus on the journey and enjoy the process. The destination will come when the time is right.

Also, don't let persistence turn into stubbornness. If you keep hitting the same wall, maybe it's time to pivot. Being persistent doesn't mean doing the same thing over and over and expecting different results. Sometimes, it's about being flexible, trying new approaches, or even reevaluating what you want.

In essence, balancing patience and persistence is all about trusting the timing of your journey while consistently putting in the effort. Keep your eyes on the prize, but don't stress over the timeline. Continue planting those seeds with dedication, nurture them with belief, and let the universe do its thing. Remember, manifesting is as much about the journey as it is about the destination. So, keep the faith, stay patient, and enjoy the beautiful unfolding of your dreams.

Practical Application: One Small Action Today

Here's the deal: big dreams are built on small actions, so let's get practical. Think of one small, manageable action you can take today that moves you closer to your goal. It doesn't have to be anything grand or life-changing—just a simple step that keeps the momentum going. Maybe it's sending that email you've been putting off, researching a new skill, or setting aside five minutes to brainstorm ideas. The key is to make it something you can do today, without a ton of effort or prep.

Once you've identified that action, commit to doing it. No overthinking, no procrastinating—just take the step. Write it down if you need to, set a reminder, or tell a friend to keep you accountable. The goal is to start building a habit of daily action, so it becomes second nature. Remember, these small steps compound over time, leading to significant progress.

Pro Tip: Do this as part of your morning routine, right after your affirmations and visualization exercises. This way, you set a positive tone for the day and keep your goals front and center. Keep it simple, keep it consistent, and watch as these small actions snowball into big changes.

7

Overcome Obstacles

Life's journey comes with its fair share of challenges and obstacles—it's just how it goes. If anyone promises they can wipe out all your problems, you should probably run the other way because that ain't gonna happen. The key is to maintain your manifesting practices even when things get tough. This chapter is here to help you anticipate potential roadblocks and navigate through them with grace. I'm going to say this one last time: manifesting works with bit-by-bit progress, not perfection. You must give yourself permission to stumble, relax, and trust that everything will be okay. The exercises and techniques you've learned are tools you can always return to whenever you're ready. It's not about doing everything perfectly; it's about practicing consistently and being kind to yourself along the way.

Learn to Let Go and Trust the Process

Let's start with the art of letting go, which can often feel like trying to balance a beach ball on your nose—awkward and tricky. In manifesting, letting go doesn't mean giving up on your desires; it means releasing your tight grip on how and when things should happen. It's about trusting the universe to do its thing, without micromanaging every detail. This is a tough pill to swallow, especially if you're a control freak who likes to plan every little detail (no judgment, we've all been there).

The beauty of letting go is that it creates space for unexpected opportunities and solutions to arise. When you're overly focused on a specific outcome or timeline, you might miss out on something even better. Think of it like this: if you're holding onto a handful of sand, the tighter you squeeze, the more it slips through your fingers. Loosen your grip, and you keep more sand in your hand. Letting go involves detaching from specific outcomes while still taking proactive steps toward your goals. It means setting your intentions clearly and taking inspired actions, but without becoming obsessed with how exactly things will unfold or when they will happen. This detachment allows you to stay open to the myriad ways the universe might deliver something even better than you imagined. It's about maintaining a balance between active participation and faith in the process, allowing for the magic of unexpected opportunities to unfold.

So, let go, relax, and trust that everything is unfolding perfectly, even if it's not exactly how you envisioned it.

Common Roadblocks

Now, let's talk about the potholes on the road to manifesting your dreams. Knowing what to expect can help you navigate these bumps more smoothly. One common roadblock is self-doubt. We're talking about that annoying voice in your head that whispers, "Can I really do this?" or "What if I fail?" Self-doubt can paralyze you, making it hard to take action or stay positive. The trick is to recognize it for what it is—a temporary feeling, not an ultimate truth. Acknowledge it, but don't let it take the driver's seat.

Another major roadblock is the fear of failure. This can be a biggie because nobody likes to fail. But here's the deal: failure is just feedback. It's not a dead-end; it's a detour offering valuable lessons. The fear of failure often stems from a perfectionist mindset, where anything less than perfect is unacceptable. Spoiler alert: perfection is a myth. It's also pretty boring. Life is messy, and that's okay.

Procrastination is another sneaky roadblock. It's easy to put off taking action, especially if the task seems daunting or uncomfortable. But procrastination is just resistance in disguise. It's a way of avoiding the discomfort of stepping out of your comfort zone. The best way to tackle procrastination is to break tasks into itty bitty, digestible steps. Kind of like what I've laid out in this book. Just focus on the next small action you can take—let go of trying to conquer the entire mountain ahead.

Strategies to Stay on Track

Staying on track with your manifesting journey can sometimes feel like herding cats—chaotic and unpredictable. But one of the most powerful strategies you can employ is learning to relax your inner voice and thoughts. This doesn't mean silencing that inner critic entirely (because, let's face it, it has a loudspeaker), but rather soothing it into a more constructive, encouraging companion.

Start by recognizing when your inner dialogue turns negative or anxious. These moments often come with self-doubt, fear, or impatience. Instead of letting these thoughts spiral, take a step back and consciously shift your perspective. Ask yourself, "Is this thought helpful? Does it serve my highest good?" If the answer is no, it's time to relax that inner voice. Imagine it as a tightly wound spring—let it unwind a little, breathe, and loosen up. This relaxation allows you to refocus on the positive aspects of your journey and the progress you've made.

Another key strategy is to remind yourself that manifesting isn't a race. It's not about how quickly you can tick off your goals but about enjoying the process and growth along the way. When you feel yourself getting caught up in deadlines or comparing your progress to others, take a deep breath and center yourself. Affirm that you're exactly where you need to be and that everything unfolds in perfect timing.

Practical techniques like mindfulness and meditation can also be invaluable here. These practices help quiet the mind and create a calm space where you can reconnect with your intentions.

Whether it's your quick 2 minute visualization exercise or a longer, guided meditation session, give yourself permission to make time to sit with your thoughts and gently guide them back to positivity and possibility.

Incorporate regular check-ins with yourself to assess your mindset and emotional state. Are you feeling overwhelmed? Anxious? Excited? Acknowledging your emotions without judgment is crucial. It's okay to feel off track sometimes; the goal is to notice it and gently steer yourself back.

It's also crucial to celebrate your wins, no matter how small. Each step forward is progress, and recognizing that helps build momentum. Whether it's treating yourself to a favorite snack or simply taking a moment to acknowledge your achievement, these little celebrations keep your spirits high and remind you why you started in the first place.

Remember, the journey of manifesting is as important as the destination. By relaxing your inner voice and staying mindful of your thoughts, you create a supportive mental environment that keeps you on track. This relaxed approach doesn't just make the process more enjoyable; it also makes you more resilient to the inevitable bumps along the way. So, give yourself the grace to relax and keep moving forward, one gentle thought at a time.

The Power of Resilience and Adaptability

Resilience and adaptability are like mastering the art of handling life's weather. Just as weather is constant—sometimes sunny, sometimes stormy—life has its ups and downs. Setbacks and challenges are inevitable; they're neither inherently good nor bad, they simply are. What makes the difference is how we perceive and respond to them.

For example, losing a job could feel like a storm cloud to some, while others might see it as a refreshing rain shower, offering a chance to pursue a new career path. It's all about perception. Just as some people enjoy the rain while others dread it, setbacks can be viewed as disasters or stepping stones, depending on the person.

Resilience means facing these inevitable storms without being overwhelmed, like a tree bending in the wind but not breaking—maintaining the strength to bounce back. Adaptability is about adjusting our plans when life's weather changes, like switching from sunglasses to an umbrella when the forecast shifts unexpectedly. This flexibility allows us to handle whatever comes our way, confident in our ability to manage the situation.

Life, like the weather, is beyond our control. Whether it's sunny or stormy, we must deal with it. Resilience helps us stand strong, while adaptability enables us to pivot and find new paths. It's not about avoiding the storm but learning to dance in the rain. By embracing these qualities, we can navigate life's unpredictability with grace and confidence, keeping our eyes on our goals while staying grounded and optimistic, no matter what the forecast holds.

Practical Application: Reflect and Adapt

For this chapter's practical application, let's focus on reflecting on recent challenges and adapting to them. This simple exercise will help you integrate the concepts of resilience and adaptability into your daily life, ensuring that you're always ready to bounce back and adjust your sails.

- Reflect on a Recent Setback: Think about a recent setback or challenge you faced. It doesn't have to be a huge life event; it could be something as simple as a plan falling through or an unexpected obstacle at work or in your personal life. Take a moment to reflect on how you felt and reacted to the situation.
- Identify the Lesson Learned: Identify one key lesson you learned from this experience. Ask yourself, "What did this situation teach me?" It could be a new perspective, a skill you gained, or simply an understanding of how to handle similar situations in the future.
- Plan Your Adaptation Strategy: Based on what you learned, consider how you can adapt your approach if a similar situation arises. For example, if you feel overwhelmed by a sudden workload increase, your adaptation strategy might be to prioritize tasks more effectively or ask for help sooner. Write down this strategy and keep it in mind for future reference.
- Incorporate Reflection into Your Weekly Routine: To reinforce these practices, set aside a few minutes at the end of each week to reflect on any challenges you encountered and how you responded. This regular reflection helps solidify your resilience and adaptability, making it easier to handle

whatever life throws your way.

52

By making this reflection and adaptation process a regular part of your routine, you're training yourself to be more resilient and adaptable. Setbacks are a natural part of life. It's how you respond to them that defines your journey.

8

Conclusion: You're Ready to Manifest Your Dream Life

Well Manifesting Maven, you've done it! Congratulations on making it to the end of *Manifesting Is Easy Peasy*! By now, you've got a solid toolkit of techniques and practices to help you manifest the life of your dreams. Always remember to stay curious and consistent. You've learned to set clear intentions, visualize your desires, cultivate a positive mindset, and take inspired actions. You've also explored the importance of letting go, trusting the process, and adapting to life's inevitable challenges.

Put It All Together

As a final practice, let's bring it all together with a quick, daily routine that encapsulates everything you've learned. This routine should take no more than six minutes most days and can easily be broken up, bit by bit, throughout your day. I invite you to even incorporate reminders or alarms throughout the day to build these habits into daily life. Here's a simple breakdown of some of these manifesting hacks:

1. Start Small and Keep It Fun: Begin with simple, enjoyable manifestations like finding a great parking spot or hearing a favorite song. (5 seconds)
2. Pen It Down: Jot down specific, clear goals, and include three aspects: Why, Feel, and Provides. Keep this memo visible to stay aligned with your intentions. (2 minutes)
3. Daily Visualization Exercise: Start your day with a 2 minute visualization of positive outcomes, mixing in visualizations of bigger life dreams. (2 minutes)
4. Develop a Positive Mindset:
5. Morning High-Five: Start your day with a quick high-five in the mirror. (2 seconds); Affirmations: Write down three affirmations that resonate with you and review them throughout the day. Reflect on these affirmations at the end of the day. (1 minute)
6. One Small Action Today: Identify one small, manageable action that moves you closer to your goal and commit to doing it. (1 minute)
7. Reflect and Adapt: Reflect on a recent setback or challenge over the past week. Identify one key lesson learned and plan an adaptation strategy. Incorporate this reflection into your weekly routine. Write it down. (5 extra minutes, once per week to start off; as you get more into it, you can build this into your daily routine and watch your manifestation magic soar exponentially!)

By incorporating these practices into your daily routine, you'll reinforce the powerful principles of manifesting and continue to attract positive experiences into your life. Keep experimenting, stay open, and most importantly, have fun with it. Thank you for joining me on this journey, and I can't wait to hear about all the amazing things you manifest. Always dream big and remember: Manifesting really *is* easy peasy... You're doing great and you've got this!

* * *

Keeping the Magic Alive

Now that you have everything you need to start manifesting with ease, it's time to pass on the good vibes and help others do the same!

By sharing your honest thoughts about this book on Amazon, you're lighting the way for future manifestors—people just like you who are curious, excited, and ready to turn their dreams into reality.

It only takes a minute, but your review could be the reason someone finally believes that they, too, have the power to manifest some magic into their lives. The more we share our experiences, the more we help others step into their own power!

Leave your review with ease. Just scan the QR code or click the link below: www.amazon.com/review/create-review/?asin=B 0DC8KPF23

Thank you for allowing me to be a part of your journey and for trusting me me to share my experience with you. The world gets brighter when we lift each other up.

    –Maura Vella

About the Author

Maura Vella is a seasoned business advisor and coach, celebrated for her unique blend of intuitive guidance and practical strategies. Known for her transformative mindset coaching and strategic planning, she empowers clients to overcome obstacles and achieve their goals. Beyond her professional achievements, Maura finds her greatest joy in being a dedicated mother to her three beautiful daughters, Sasha, Shira, and Summer.

www.ingramcontent.com/pod-product-compliance
Lightning Source LLC
Chambersburg PA
CBHW061718130726
47996CB00006B/2384